The Furrtails

By Shandi Finnessey

Illustrated by Cathi Wong

ISBN 0-7414-1197-0

Published by:

INFINITY
PUBLISHING.COM

1094 New DeHaven Street, Suite 100
West Conshohocken, PA 19428-2713
Info@buybooksontheweb.com
www.buybooksontheweb.com
Toll-free (877) BUY BOOK
Local Phone (610) 941-9999
Fax (610) 941-9959

Printed in the United States of America
Printed on Recycled Paper
Published March 2005

Dedication

It is not only the pages in this book
but also the pages of my life
that I dedicate to my parents,
Linda and Patrick,
two extraordinary individuals
that have taught me through demonstration
to find the things that are

"special"

in all of us.

Once upon a time, deep in the lush green valley of Carrotville, lived a family of rabbits named the Furrtails. There was Mama and Papa Furrtail, and their two sons, Sammy and Robby.

They enjoyed having their burrow next to Mr. Villman's farm. Each year Mr. Villman won the blue ribbon at the county fair for his delicious prize winning carrots. The Furrtails made sure to enjoy these blue ribbon carrots as well.

One morning in early summer, Robby Furrtail grabbed an old sack and headed out over the field to Mr. Villman's farm to gather some fresh carrots for afternoon snacking. As he hopped across the yard, his older brother Sammy went hopping after him. "Wait for me," Sammy shouted across the yard. Robby stopped and sighed, "You're always so slow, Sammy. If you want to come with me, you've got to keep up."

As the two bounded across the grass, Mrs. Furrtail's voice could be heard across the yard. "Robby, Sammy, now remember to stay together and look out for each other."

The two rabbits hopped through the grass, over the hills and streams, and squirmed their fuzzy bodies under fences, until finally they stood at the edge of Mr. Villman's farm. "Wow! Look at all that food!" exclaimed Sammy as he gazed at the rows of lettuce, carrots, and other delicious treats.

Robby hopped ahead of Sammy, rushing from row to row,

gathering as many plump carrots and crisp heads of lettuce his sack

could carry. He gave no care to his older brother as he tasted some

of the treats from his bag.

Meanwhile, Sammy began to wander through the many rows of

vegetables when something suddenly caught his eye. It was the

largest, juiciest looking carrot Sammy had ever seen, and it was just

lying by itself inside some funny looking box. Sammy had to taste

that delicious looking carrot. He hopped toward the box and slowly

stepped inside.

10

He could already smell the sweetness of the carrot and his

mouth began to water as he approached his meal. Just as Sammy sank

his teeth into his bright orange treat, "BANG," the door slammed shut

behind him, trapping him inside the box. Sammy ran from corner to

corner inside the cage, searching for an opening, but it was no use. He

was stuck. Sammy sat down and began to cry.

At the other edge of the farm, Robby had filled his sack with fresh vegetables and was beginning to look around for Sammy. "Oh, where could he be now?" Robby asked himself while hopping up and down the rows searching for his older brother. He looked and looked, but could not find Sammy, and it had started to get dark. "Maybe he decided to go home," Robby thought, and he headed back through the grass, over the hills and streams, and under the fences until he finally reached the Furrtails burrow.

Robby pulled his sack inside and sat down to eat a snack of carrots. Mrs. Furrtail appeared in the doorway. "Good, I am glad you are home. It is beginning to get dark. Where is Sammy?" Robby looked up. "But... I thought he was here." "You mean he didn't come home with you?" Mrs. Furrtail was beginning to panic. "Come, we must find him before it gets too dark. Where is the last place you saw him?" "At Mr. Villman's farm," Robby exclaimed as he jumped up, hopped out of the burrow, and bounded through the yard, Mrs. Furrtail close behind.

"You know, Robby, you really should have kept a closer watch on Sammy." "But I don't understand. He is two years older than me. Why can't he do the same things that I can?" Mrs. Furrtail stopped running and turned toward Robby. "We all have things that we are really good at and things that we need help with. Some things that you are good at, I am not. And some things that I am good at, you are not. That is what makes us all special."

Robby thought about this for a moment. "What can you do, Mom, that I cannot?" Mrs. Furrtail chuckled and replied, "Well, do you know how to bake a carrot cake? Or how about patch a hole in a pair of jeans?" Robby smiled. "I think I understand. I am very good at running fast and hopping high into the air. Sammy is good at drawing pretty pictures, telling funny jokes, and helping you around the house. We are different, but we are both very special." "That's right, dear. And you are both very special to me. So let's go find your brother."

20

Robby and Mrs. Furrtail hopped through the grass, over the hills

and streams, and squirmed their fuzzy bodies under fences, until they

finally stood at the edge of Mr. Villmer's farm. The sky had turned a

dark shade of blue, and the rows of vegetables were dark with

shadows. "It's scary out here, Mom," Robby said, his eyes wide with

fear. "I know, dear. Just stay close to me. We must find him before

Mr. Villman does," Mrs. Furrtail said as she hopped toward the dark

rows of vegetables.

Robby and Mrs. Furrtail hopped quietly up and down the rows as

twisted vines reached at their legs. The only light came from the full

moon, high in the darkened sky. Robby and Mrs. Furrtail began to run

fast, searching down each row for Sammy. "Sammy. Can you hear me?

Where are you?" Mrs. Furrtail whispered into the darkness.

"Mom, is that you?" Sammy shouted into the night. "I'm over here, stuck in this dumb box." Mrs. Furrtail and Robby hurried to where Sammy's voice was coming from, and found him trapped inside a cage. Robby ran to the cage and pulled with all of his strength, trying to lift the trap door. It was useless. There was a lock on the top of the cage and the door was much too heavy for Robby.

"Hey, Robby, I drew you a picture while I was stuck in this box all day," Sammy said, holding out the picture. "I don't have time for this now, Sammy." Robby was beginning to become angry. Mrs. Furrtail walked over to Sammy and glanced down at the picture. "Um, Robby, I think you may want to take a look at this. It may be exactly what we need," exclaimed Mrs. Furrtail excitedly. Sammy had drawn a plan for his escape!

The Furrtails went straight to work. Sammy told his mother and

brother exactly what to do from the plan he drew in his picture. Mrs.

Furrtail gathered some grass and knitted a long rope. Robby jumped

high into the air and landed on top of the box so that he could unlock

the latch. They tied the rope onto the trap door, and together Mrs.

Furrtail and Robby pulled with all of their strength. Slowly, the door

began to move.

When the door was open wide enough, Sammy crawled from the

cage. "WE DID IT!" they all cried. Together, the Furrtails were able

to free Sammy from the trap by using all their special traits.

Without one of the Furrtails, they would not have been able to get

Sammy out.

Sammy, Robby, and Mrs. Furrtail hugged each other and walked

home together, across the fields, through the grass, over the hills

and streams, and under the fences until they finally reached the

Furrtails burrow.

The End

Suggested Activities:

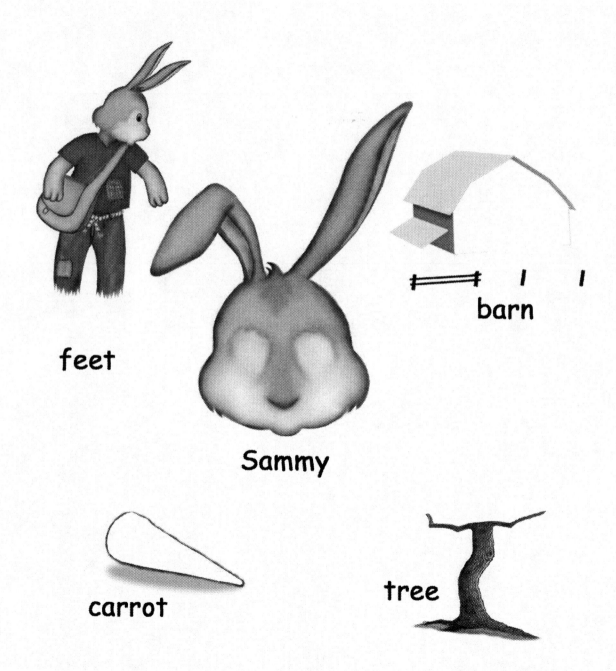

feet

barn

Sammy

carrot

tree

38

Sammy is good at drawing pictures. Help Sammy finish these pictures. Draw what is missing in each picture. What kind of pictures can you draw?

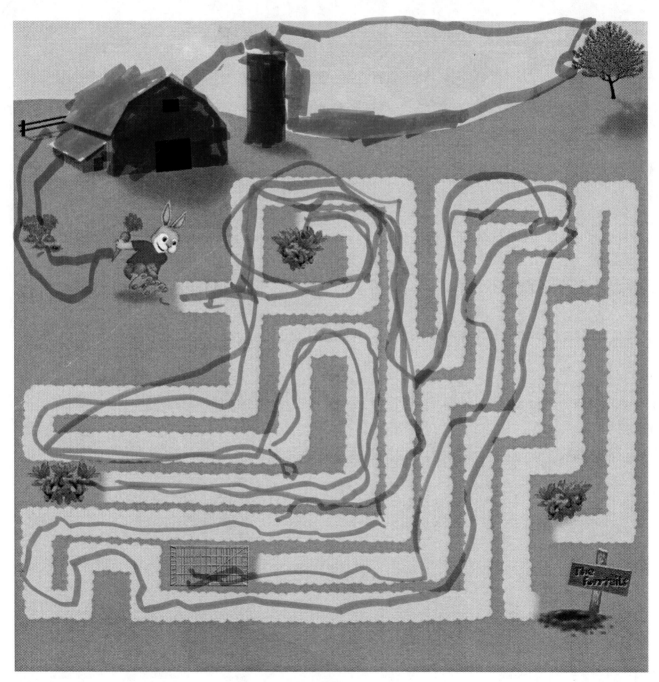

40

Robby is good at running fast. Help Robby run home from Mr.

Villman's farm. Be sure to watch out for the lettuce patches and the

cage!

Robby

Sammy

42

Mrs. Furrtail is good at patching holes in Robby and Sammy's jeans.

Help Mrs. Furrtail match the patches to the holes in Sammy's jeans.

Color the patches on Robby's jeans.

Mr. Villman has lost some items. Help him find them. Circle the words

you find. They can be up or down, across, vertical, or even backwards!

vegetable
carrot
lettuce
row
blue ribbon
fair
farm
rabbit
cage
Furrtail
Robby
Sammy
burrow

```
A  M  V  I  F  L  O  R  G  E  V
E  L  E  T  C  A  R  O  W  B  G
R  I  B  F  A  I  R  W  C  A  W
O  T  I  V  R  O  T  M  I  Y  H
B  L  U  E  R  I  B  B  O  N  E
R  I  B  V  O  N  F  B  A  T  A
V  E  G  E  T  A  B  L  E  B  U
S  G  T  L  T  T  B  A  T  U  T
T  A  E  C  U  T  T  E  L  R  T
E  C  M  T  L  P  I  E  S  R  O
T  E  R  M  E  R  B  T  M  O  R
L  F  U  R  Y  B  B  O  R  W  U
A  C  L  E  V  T  A  L  R  B  B
M  O  R  F  U  R  R  T  A  I  L
S  Y  H  N  A  I  B  N  F  D  I
```

Shandi Finnessey, Miss USA 2004, is a graduate student in St. Louis, Missouri, working toward her doctorate degree in counseling. She is an advocate for individuals with mental challenges and gives of her heart, her voice, and her time to integrating these individuals into society.

In her free time, she enjoys practicing meditation and yoga, painting abstracts, practicing the piano and violin, and playing with her cat, Squeaky, and her bird, Sunny.

Cathi (Cat) Wong is a fourth generation Californian and resident of San Francisco. She graduated from City College of San Francisco and the University of San Francisco with degrees in business and organizational behavior, respectively. After completing her corporate tour of duty, (adding electro-mechanical drafting credentials to her resume along the way), she grew anxious for greener pastures and, seven years ago, found her bliss freelancing in the world of illustrating and design.

Cat enjoys working and playing independently as an artist, wife, mother, friend to those in need, and caretaker of two delightful water turtles, Donni and Meiki.